Tropical Drinks and Pupus
FROM HAWAII

*H*awaiian "pupus" are appetizers and they are marvelous. They come hot, cold, hearty . . . large or small . . . do-ahead or do-your-own. Guests often bring them as "hostess gifts" to cocktail parties.

These luscious hors d'oeuvres represent Island cuisine at its exotic best. Variety is unlimited because most are Heritage recipes from Hawaii's multi-ethnic creative cooks.

Serve them with Island-style Tropical Drinks . . . spirited, inspired, party pleasers.

Try it. Give an original Pupu Party instead of just a cocktail hour. Your guests will love it.

This Island Heritage book will show you how.

Aloha.

1

Table of Contents

Bougainvillea

TROPICAL DRINKS

Cymbidium

Coconut Calabash

1½ ounces light rum
 1 ounce coconut cream
½ ounce Cointreau
½ ounce orgeat
    Cracked ice

Blend together rum, coconut cream, Cointreau and orgeat. Pour into a serving container filled with cracked ice. Serve with straws. Makes 1 serving.

Idea: Saw off the top third of a fresh husked coconut to use as a serving container. After the first use scrape out the coconut meat and save the container.

Chi Chi

1 wedge fresh pineapple
3 ounces pineapple juice
3 ounces vodka
1 ounce coconut syrup
½ ounce fresh lemon juice
1 cup cracked ice

Process fresh pineapple in a blender until smooth. Add pineapple juice, vodka, coconut syrup, lemon juice and cracked ice; blend well. Pour into stemmed glasses. Makes 2 servings.

Idea: Garnish with fresh pineapple wedge, vanda orchid and a sprig of fresh mint.

Mai Tai

1½ ounces light rum
 ½ ounce dark rum
 ½ ounce orange curacao
 ½ ounce fresh lime juice
 ½ ounce Hawaiian Cane Syrup
 ¼ ounce orgeat syrup
    Cracked ice
 1 ounce Lemon Hart rum (86)

In a double old fashioned glass combine light rum, dark rum, curacao, lime juice, Hawaiian Cane Syrup and orgeat syrup; stir well. Fill glass with cracked ice. Gently pour Lemon Hart rum on top to float on surface. Makes 1 drink.

Idea: Garnish with fresh pineapple wedge, vanda orchid and a sprig of fresh mint.

Hawaiian Cane Syrup

Combine equal amounts of sugar and water and bring to a boil. Boil 5 minutes, stirring constantly. Chill.

The Royal Pineapple

  1 small fresh pineapple
1½ ounces light rum
  3 ounces pineapple juice
 ½ ounce fresh lemon juice
  1 teaspoon Hawaiian Cane Syrup
     Cracked ice

Cut off the top of the pineapple about 1-inch below the crown. Hollow out the cavity, leaving ½-inch of the fruit inside the rind. Reserve fresh fruit for other uses. Cut a notch in the crown. Blend together rum, pineapple juice, lemon juice and Hawaiian Cane Syrup. Fill the pineapple container with cracked ice and pour in the rum mixture. Top pineapple with the crown and insert two straws through the notch. Makes 1 drink.

Blue Hawaii

1½ ounces light rum
1½ ounces pineapple juice
  1 ounce blue curacao
  1 ounce fresh lemon juice
     Small cube fresh pineapple
  1 cup cracked ice

Combine rum, pineapple juice, blue curacao, lemon juice and pineapple in a blender. Process until smooth. Gradually add cracked ice; blend well. Pour into two chilled stemmed glasses. Makes 2 drinks.

Kona Gold

2 ounces light rum
Juice of ½ a lemon
1 ounce orange juice
½ ounce curacao
1 teaspoon Hawaiian Cane Syrup
Cracked ice

Place all ingredients in a container filled with cracked ice and shake well to blend. Strain into a chilled cocktail glass. Makes 1 drink.

Plantation Punch

2 ounces dark rum
1 tablespoon fresh lime juice
½ ounce grenadine
1 teaspoon Hawaiian Cane Syrup
Ice cubes
Club soda, chilled

Pour rum, lime juice, grenadine and Hawaiian Cane Syrup into a tall glass and stir. Fill with ice cubes. Pour in club soda. Makes 1 drink.

Mango Daiquiri

1 large ripe mango, peeled and seeded
3 ounces light rum
½ ounce fresh lemon juice
1 ounce Hawaiian Cane Syrup
2 cups cracked ice

Combine mango, rum, lemon juice and Hawaiian Cane Syrup in a blender; process until smooth. Gradually add cracked ice; blend well. Pour into two chilled daiquiri glasses. Makes 2 drinks.

Banana Daiquiri

1 large banana, cut into chunks
3 ounces light rum
1 teaspoon fresh lime juice
2 teaspoons Hawaiian Cane Syrup
2 cups cracked ice

Combine banana, rum, lime juice and Hawaiian Cane Syrup in a blender; process until smooth. Gradually add cracked ice; blend well. Pour into two chilled daiquiri glasses. Makes 2 drinks.

Pineapple Mint Daiquiri

1 cup fresh pineapple chunks
1 tablespoon chopped mint
3 ounces light rum
1 tablespoon Hawaiian Cane Syrup
2 cups cracked ice

Combine pineapple, mint, rum and Hawaiian Cane Syrup in a blender; process until smooth. Gradually add cracked ice; blend well. Pour into two chilled daiquiri glasses. Makes 2 drinks.

Idea: Garnish with a sprig of fresh mint and a vanda orchid.

Aloha Gimlet

1½ ounces vodka
1 ounce lime juice
1 ounce water
Cracked ice

Blend together vodka, lime juice and water. Pour into a gimlet glass filled with cracked ice. Garnish with a vanda orchid, if desired. Makes 1 drink.

The Honolulu

3 ounces gin
2 ounces pineapple juice
2 ounces orange juice
  Squeeze of fresh lemon juice
  A few drops of grenadine
  Cracked ice

Place all ingredients in a container filled with cracked ice and shake well to blend. Strain into a chilled cocktail glasses. Makes 2 servings.

Idea: Garnish with a lemon twist and a sprig of fresh mint.

Singapore Sling

1½ ounces gin
1 ounce sloe gin
½ ounce cherry brandy
1 tablespoon fresh lemon juice
2 ounces water
  Ice cubes

Blend together gin, sloe gin, cherry brandy, lemon juice and water. Pour into a tall glass filled with ice cubes. Makes 1 drink.

Hawaiian Cooler

    4 ounces pineapple juice
1 ½ ounces bourbon
     Juice of ½ a lime
     Cracked ice

Blend together pineapple juice, bourbon and lime juice. Pour into a glass filled with cracked ice. Makes 1 serving.

Kamaaina Kooler

1 can (6 oz.) orange-passion fruit juice concentrate
1 can (6 oz.) guava nectar concentrate
1 bottle (28 oz.) club soda, chilled
  Maraschino cherries
  Pineapple wedges
  Ice cubes

Combine orange-passion fruit juice and guava nectar in a punch bowl or pitcher. Stir in club soda. Add cherries and pineapple wedges. Serve over ice cubes or with a decorative ice ring, if desired. Makes 8 (5 oz.) servings.

PARADISE PUNCHES

Plumeria

Tropical Punch

Tropical Ice Ring
4 bottles (750 ml. each) chablis, well chilled
1½ bottles (750 ml. each) dark rum, well chilled
1½ cups brandy, well chilled
1½ cups fresh lime juice, well chilled
4 cups pineapple juice, well chilled

When ready to serve unmold the Tropical Ice Ring into a punch bowl and pour over the chablis, rum, brandy, lime juice and pineapple juice. Makes 50 (4 oz.) servings.

Tropical Ice Ring

Pineapple juice
Chunks of fresh pineapple
Strawberries
Green grapes
Vanda orchids
Sprigs of fresh mint

In a bowl or mold pour in pineapple juice in a thin layer and freeze. Add remaining ingredients a few pieces at a time and a little more pineapple juice; freeze. Continue this process for several days, so that the ingredients are suspended throughout.

Mai Tai Punch

1 small fresh pineapple
1 basket strawberries
2 bottles (750 ml. each) mai tai mix without
  alcohol
1 bottle (750 ml.) brandy
1 bottle (750 ml.) light rum
1½ quarts orange juice
  Sprigs of mint

Remove rind and core from pineapple and cut fruit into cubes; freeze. Remove stems from strawberries; freeze. Chill all the remaining ingredients. When ready to serve pour mai tai mix, brandy, rum and orange juice into a punch bowl. Float the frozen pineapple cubes and strawberries in the punch. Garnish with sprigs of fresh mint. Makes 30 (5 oz.) servings.

Coconut Island Punch

2 cans (12 oz. each) coconut milk, chilled
¼ cup Hawaiian Cane Syrup
1 can (46 oz.) pineapple juice, chilled
1 bottle (750 ml.) light rum
2 tablespoons lemon juice
  Frozen cubes of fresh pineapple or ice cubes

In a punch bowl combine coconut milk, Hawaiian Cane Syrup, pineapple juice, light rum and lemon juice; stir well. When ready to serve add frozen pineapple cubes. Makes 20 (5 oz.) servings.

Pineapple Calabash Punch

1 **fresh pineapple**
3 **tablespoons sugar**
¼ **cup brandy**
2 **cans (46 oz. each) pineapple juice**
½ **gallon white wine, chilled**

Remove rind and core from pineapple; chop fruit. Sprinkle sugar on chopped pineapple; stir in brandy and marinate in refrigerator for six hours or overnight. Combine fruit and juice; refrigerate. Add wine just before serving. Makes 50 (4 oz.) servings.

Kamaaina Wine Punch

1 **bottle (750 ml.) sparkling white wine**
2 **ounces Cognac**
2 **ounces Grand Marnier**
   Zest of an orange, cut in strips
   Zest of a lemon, cut in strips
1 **tablespoon sugar**
2 **bottles (8 oz. each) club soda, chilled**
   Ice cubes

In a 2-quart pitcher combine wine, Cognac, Grand Marnier, orange zest, lemon zest and sugar; blend well. Chill 2 to 3 hours. When ready to serve add club soda and ice cubes; stir gently. Makes 12 (4 oz.) servings.

Margarita Punch

4 bottles (750 ml. each) tequila
1 bottle (750 ml.) triple sec
1 quart fresh lime juice
4 bottles (750 ml. each) champagne
1 egg white
2 tablespoons water
  Coarse salt for glasses
  Ice Ring

Chill tequila, triple sec, lime juice and champagne. Beat together egg white and water. Dip the rim of the serving glasses in egg mixture, then into the salt. Let dry. When ready to serve place the ice ring in a punch bowl and pour in the chilled tequila, triple sec, lime juice and champagne. Serve in salt rimmed glasses. Makes 50 (5 oz.) servings.

Haleakala Deep Freeze

1 can (6 oz.) lemonade or limeade concentrate
12 ounces vodka
6 ounces water
  Cracked ice
  Lemon twists
  Sprigs of mint

Combine lemonade, vodka and water in a blender. Fill blender with cracked ice; blend well. Pour into chilled glasses and garnish with lemon twists and sprigs of mint. Makes 6 servings.

Island Punch Bowl

3 cups pineapple chunks
4 oranges, peeled and sectioned
1 quart orange juice
2 cans (6 oz. each) guava nectar
2 bottles (28 oz.) club soda
  Sprigs of mint

Chill the pineapple, oranges, orange juice, guava nectar
and club soda. When ready to serve place all the chilled
ingredients in a punch bowl. Serve a few pieces of the fruit
in each glass. Garnish with sprigs of mint. Makes 20 (5
oz.) servings.

Keiki Sangria

1 lemon, cut into ¼-inch slices
1 orange, cut into ¼-inch slices
¼ cup sugar
1 quart tropical fruit punch
1 can (46 oz.) pineapple juice
1 bottle (28 oz.) club soda, chilled
  Ice ring decorated with lemon slices, orange
    slices and mint

Combine lemon slices, orange slices and sugar; mix well.
Add tropical fruit punch and pineapple juice. Refrigerate
for at least 2 or 3 hours or until thoroughly chilled. When
ready to serve pour juice mixture into a punch bowl. Add
club soda and decorated ice ring. Makes 24 (4 oz.) servings.

Pineapple Cooler

1 quart pineapple juice
2 cups apple juice
½ cup fresh lemon juice
1 quart pineapple sherbet
  Sprigs of fresh mint

Blend together pineapple juice, apple juice and lemon juice
and chill in the freezer until ice crystals just start to form.
Place glasses in freezer to become frosted. When ready to
serve place scoops of pineapple sherbet in individual glasses
and pour in the chilled juices. Garnish with sprigs of mint.
Serve immediately. Makes 12 servings.

Beach Boy Punch

1 quart orange juice
1 quart cranberry juice
¼ cup lemon juice
2 bottles (28 oz. each) gingerale
  Frozen ice ring or cubes of cranberry juice

Chill orange juice, cranberry juice, lemon juice and gingerale. When ready to serve place the ice ring or cubes of
cranberry juice in a punch bowl. Pour in the orange juice,
cranberry juice and lemon juice. Just before serving add
the gingerale. Makes 30 (4 oz.) servings.

Idea: Rum or vodka added to this recipe makes a special
party punch.

MADAME PELE SIZZLERS

Anthurium

Green Peppercorn Steak
with Mango Chutney Sauce

      3 **pound sirloin steak, 1-inch thick**
      ¼ **cup green peppercorns**
      ½ **cup clarified butter**
      ⅓ **cup butter**
      ½ **cup brandy or cognac**
      1 **cup heavy cream**
      ½ **cup coarsely chopped mango chutney**
         Salt

Cut sirloin steak into 1-inch cubes. Coarsely grind the green peppercorns and place them in a large plastic bag; add beef cubes and toss until well coated. Heat ¼ cup of the clarified butter in a heavy skillet until very hot. Brown half the beef cubes in the skillet for a few minutes over high heat, remove meat and keep warm in a 200F. oven. Add the remaining ¼ cup of the clarified butter to the skillet and brown the remaining meat and keep warm. Add the ⅓ cup butter to the pan juices; stir in brandy. Bring to a boil, then immediately reduce heat to a simmer. Stir in heavy cream and mango chutney; simmer until thickened. Season to taste with salt. Pour the sauce over the beef cubes to serve. Makes 10 to 12 servings.

Adobo (Filipino Spiced Pork)

    2 pounds lean pork
    1 cup Japanese rice vinegar
    ½ cup soy sauce
    3 cloves garlic, thinly sliced
    6 peppercorns
    1 bay leaf
    2 tablespoons oil

Cut pork into 1-inch cubes. In a heavy skillet combine rice vinegar, soy sauce, garlic, peppercorns and bay leaf; bring to a boil, reduce heat and simmer for 15 minutes. Add pork and cover; simmer, stirring occasionally, until pork is tender, about 1 hour. Remove pork and garlic from sauce. Heat oil in a skillet and stir fry pork and garlic over high heat for a few minutes. Serve hot. Makes 8 to 10 servings.

Sweet and Sour Cocktail Sausages

    1 cup pineapple juice
    ½ cup vinegar
    2 teaspoons soy sauce
    ¾ cup brown sugar
    2 teaspoons dry mustard
    1½ tablespoons cornstarch
    2 pkgs. (5 oz. each) cocktail sausages

In a small saucepan combine pineapple juice, vinegar, soy sauce, brown sugar, dry mustard and cornstarch. Bring to a boil, stirring constantly; reduce heat and simmer until sauce thickens. Stir sausages into sauce and cook for 10 minutes or until heated through. Makes 6 to 8 servings.

Lemon Chicken Bits

3 whole boneless chicken breasts
¼ cup chicken stock
2 tablespoons dry sherry
1 clove garlic, finely chopped
  Pinch of salt
¾ cup flour
2 cups cornstarch
1 cup cold water
1 tablespoon sesame oil
4 cups oil
  Lemon Sauce
  Shredded cabbage or lettuce

Remove skin from chicken and cut into 1-inch cubes. In a bowl combine chicken, chicken stock, sherry, garlic and salt. Marinate chicken for 30 minutes. Prepare batter by combining flour, 1 cup of the cornstarch, cold water and sesame oil; blend until smooth. Let stand 20 to 30 minutes. Remove chicken from the marinade and coat with the remaining 1 cup of the cornstarch. The easiest way is to place the cornstarch in a plastic bag, drop a few pieces of chicken into the bag and shake until the chicken is well coated. Heat oil in a wok or heavy pan to 300F. The chicken will be cooked again at a higher temperature just before serving. Drop the coated chicken into the batter, then into the hot oil and cook for 2 to 3 minutes. When ready to serve raise the temperature of the oil to 375F. and drop the chicken, a handful at a time, into the hot oil. The chicken will be very crisp. Drain on absorbent paper towels. Prepare Lemon Sauce recipe. Cover a large platter with shredded cabbage. Place the chicken on the platter and top with some of the lemon sauce. Serve with the remaining sauce in a bowl. Makes 10 to 12 servings.

Idea: Garnish with thin lemon wedges and sprigs of Chinese parsley.

Lemon Sauce

2 cups rich chicken stock
½ cup fresh lemon juice
¾ cup sugar
   Zest of a lemon, finely chopped
¼ cup cornstarch
¼ cup water

In a wok or saucepan bring chicken stock to a boil; add lemon juice, sugar and lemon zest. Return mixture to a boil. Blend together cornstarch and water and stir into the lemon sauce. Cook until thickened, stirring frequently. Adjust seasoning. Makes 3 cups.

Rumaki

6 chicken livers (about ½ pound)
12 water chestnuts
12 slices bacon
3 tablespoons soy sauce
1 teaspoon sugar
½ teaspoon minced fresh ginger

Cut chicken livers into quarters. Slice water chestnuts and bacon in half. Combine soy sauce, sugar and ginger; marinate chicken livers for 20 minutes. Wrap a piece of chicken liver and a piece of water chestnut in each bacon strip and secure with a food pick. Broil 4 inches from heat, turning occasionally, for about 10 minutes or until bacon is crisp. Food picks may be replaced before serving. Makes 24.

Korean Fried Mandoo

½ head cabbage, chopped
8 ounces bean sprouts, rinsed and drained
½ pound ground pork
2 green onions, thinly sliced
1 clove garlic, minced
1 tablespoon soy sauce
2 teaspoons sesame oil
¼ teaspoon pepper
   Oil for deep frying
36 wun tun wrappers
   Korean Dipping Sauce

Simmer cabbage in ½ cup water for 5 minutes; drain. Place in a cloth and squeeze out excess water. Simmer bean sprouts in ½ cup water for 2 minutes; drain. Place in a cloth and squeeze out excess water; chop. Combine cabbage, bean sprouts, pork, green onions, garlic, soy sauce, sesame oil and pepper; mix well. Heat oil for deep frying to 375F. Place 1 tablespoon of the filling mixture in the center of a wun tun wrapper. Brush edges of wrapper with water and fold into a rectangle. Fry in oil until golden brown on both sides. Drain on absorbent paper. Serve hot with Korean Dipping Sauce. Makes 36.

Idea: If preferred, pork can be precooked slightly before combining with remaining ingredients.

Korean Dipping Sauce

½ cup soy sauce
¼ cup vinegar
2 teaspoons paprika
½ teaspoon pepper
1 teaspoon minced fresh ginger or ¼ teaspoon powdered ginger
2 cloves garlic, minced
3 green onions, thinly sliced
¼ cup brown sugar

Combine all ingredients; mix well. Makes 1 cup.

Polynesian Shrimp Toast

6 slices day old white bread
½ pound shrimp, shelled and deveined
1 egg white
2 teaspoons sherry
2 teaspoons cornstarch
¼ cup finely chopped water chestnuts
1 tablespoon thinly sliced green onions
1 teaspoon minced fresh ginger
½ teaspoon salt
2 tablespoon sesame seeds
    Oil for shallow frying

Trim crust from bread, then cut into four triangles. Mince shrimp. Beat egg white until foamy, then stir in sherry and cornstarch. Add shrimp, water chestnuts, green onions, ginger and salt; mix well. Spread 2 teaspoons of shrimp mixture over each triangle. Sprinkle each triangle with ¼ teaspoon sesame seeds and press them in firmly. Cover and refrigerate until ready to cook. Heat oil in a wok or frying pan to 350F. Fry triangles, shrimp side down, for 1 to 1½ minutes or until one side is golden brown. Turn over and fry an additional 1 to 1½ minutes. Drain on absorbent paper. Keep warm in a 200F. oven until ready to serve. Makes 24.

Idea: Shrimp toast can be made ahead, then frozen. To reheat, bake at 350F. for 10 to 15 minutes or until hot and crisp.

Gingered Shrimp

2 pounds shrimp (15 to 20 count)
½ cup butter
½ cup finely chopped green onion
¼ cup finely chopped fresh ginger
2 cloves garlic, minced
¼ cup finely chopped parsley
   Salt and freshly ground black pepper

Clean shrimp and remove shells, leaving tails intact. In a heavy skillet heat the butter and saute the shrimp until they are pink. Remove shrimp from the skillet and set aside. Add green onion, ginger and garlic; saute for 2 to 3 minutes. Add the shrimp, toss well, sprinkle with parsley. Season to taste with salt and pepper. Serve with thinly sliced French bread, if desired. Makes 10 to 12 servings.

Koko Crater Mushrooms

24 mushrooms
1 pound fresh spinach
½ cup grated parmesan cheese
4 ounces crumbled feta cheese
½ cup chopped green onion
½ cup chopped parsley

Preheat oven to 400F. Clean mushrooms and remove stems. Blanch spinach; drain and coarsely chop. Combine spinach, parmesan cheese, feta cheese, green onion and parsley; blend well. Fill the mushroom caps with the mixture. The mixture may be made into small balls and frozen until you are ready to prepare the baked mushrooms, then just place the cheese balls into the mushroom caps. Bake for 10 minutes. If cheese is frozen, bake 15 minutes. Makes 24.

Pacific Crab and Cheese Tarts

   3 eggs
1½ cups heavy cream
   1 teaspoon Dijon style mustard
  ½ teaspoon salt
  ¼ teaspoon white pepper
   1 cup crab, coarsely chopped
  ¾ cup grated Swiss cheese
 24 baked Tart Shells (recipe follows)

Preheat oven to 350F. Combine eggs, heavy cream, mustard, salt and white pepper in a food processor or bowl; mix well. Stir in crab and Swiss cheese. Fill the baked tart shells with the crab mixture. Replace filled tart shells in muffin tins and bake for 12 minutes or until the filling is set. Makes 24.

Tart Shells

  ½ cup cold butter
1½ cups flour
   1 teaspoon dill weed
   1 teaspoon thyme
  ½ teaspoon salt
  ¼ teaspoon white pepper
  ⅓ cup cold water

In a food processor or by hand blend together the butter and flour until the size of cornmeal. Stir in the dill weed, thyme, salt and white pepper. Add the water and mix until the dough forms a ball. Chill for 30 minutes. When ready to bake preheat oven to 375F. Sprinkle a pastry cloth or board wtih a little flour. Turn the dough out and roll ⅛-inch thick. Cut the dough the size of a flattened muffin paper and place the dough in a muffin paper lined muffin tin. Bake for 8 to 10 minutes. The shells may be prepared ahead of time and stored in an airtight container. Makes 24.

Island Meatballs with Curry Dip

½ pound ground beef
½ pound ground pork
½ pound ground veal or turkey meat
½ cup chopped onions
 2 eggs
 1 cup fresh bread crumbs
 2 cloves garlic, finely chopped
½ cup chopped parsley
    Salt and pepper to taste
    Curry Dip

Combine all ingredients, except Curry Dip; mix well. Shape into meatballs, about 1-inch in diameter. Bake meatballs on a baking sheet, uncovered, for 20 minutes at 350F. or microwave for 10 minutes at high power. Meatballs may be made ahead and frozen. Reheat before serving. Serve with Curry Dip. Makes 60.

Curry Dip

 1 cup plain yogurt
 1 teaspoon curry powder
 3 tablespoons chopped fresh mint

Combine all ingredients; mix well. Chill. Serve as a dipping sauce for Island Meatballs. Makes 1 cup.

Fried Ginger Pork

 2 pounds lean pork
¼ cup oil
 1 cup finely minced Maui onion
 2 cloves garlic, minced
½ cup soy sauce
 1 tablespoon chopped fresh ginger
 2 tablespoons vinegar
 1 tablespoon toasted sesame seeds

Cut the pork into 1-inch cubes. Heat oil in a heavy skillet
and saute pork on all sides, until brown. Add onions and
garlic and cook for 5 minutes. Stir in soy sauce, ginger and
vinegar; cover the pan and simmer for 10 minutes. Sprinkle sesame seeds over the pork and serve with foodpicks
as a pupu.

Spicy Macadamia Nut Nibbles

 2 tablespoons butter
 2 cups macadamia nuts
½ teaspoon garlic salt
 1 tablespoon soy sauce
   Dash of chili powder

Preheat oven to 300F. Melt butter on a baking sheet, then
spread macadamia nuts on the baking sheet and bake for
about 20 minutes, stirring often. Remove macadamia nuts
from the oven and sprinkle with garlic salt, soy sauce and
chili powder. Cool and store in an air tight container.
Makes 2 cups.

TRADEWIND
APPETIZERS

Cattleya Orchid

Madame Pele Cocktail Sauce

1 cup ketchup
¼ cup chopped kim chee
½ teaspoon Worcestershire sauce
2 teaspoons lemon juice
2 drops hot pepper sauce

Combine all ingredients. Chill. Excellent as a dip for chilled shrimp and crab. Makes 1½ cups.

Chilled Lobster in Tart Shells

1½ cups cooked lobster, cubed
¾ to 1 cup mayonnaise
1 small clove garlic, minced
½ teaspoon dry mustard
1 teaspoon tarragon
1 teaspoon capers, chopped
1 tablespoon finely chopped sour pickles
18 baked Tart Shells (recipe page 31)
Parsley

Place lobster in a small bowl and blend in mayonnaise until moistened. Stir in garlic, dry mustard, tarragon, capers and sour pickles. Chill until ready to use. Fill baked tart shells with the crab mixture. Garnish each with a small sprig of parsley. Makes 18.

Idea: Substitute crab meat for the lobster.

Pacific Smoked Salmon Spread

1 pkg. (8 oz.) cream cheese, softened
1 pkg. (3 oz.) smoked salmon, cubed
1 teaspoon lemon juice
1 tablespoon chopped onion
1 tablespoon thinly sliced green onion

Combine cream cheese, salmon, lemon juice and onion; mix until well blended. Sprinkle with green onion. Serve with crisp crackers or melba toast. Makes 6 to 8 servings.

Ewa Chicken Liver Pate

  1 **pound chicken livers**
 ¼ **cup chopped green onion**
 ¼ **pound mushrooms, cleaned**
 ¼ **cup parsley**
 ½ **teaspoon salt**
 ½ **teaspoon thyme**
  2 **tablespoons brandy**
  1 **cup unsalted butter, room temperature**
    Clarified butter

Place the chicken livers in a saucepan and add cold water to cover. Add green onion and bring to a boil; reduce heat and simmer for 5 minutes. Turn off the heat and allow chicken livers to sit for 5 minutes. Drain the chicken livers and place them in a food processor; process until very smooth. Add the remaining ingredients, except clarified butter, and process again until smooth. If a very smooth mixture is desired, then strain through a medium mesh. Pour the mixture into a serving container. Pour a very thin layer of clarified butter over the top of the pate to keep it from drying out. Chill for several hours or overnight. Serve with fresh melba toast. Makes 6 servings.

Idea #1: When pate is firm make cut out decorations using thin pieces of black olives, egg white, carrot or thin slices of vegetables. You can make flowers or other designs on the pate, then carefully pour a very thin layer of clarified butter over the top.

Idea #2: For a spicier pate add 1 teaspoon horseradish and 1 teaspoon Dijon style mustard to the above recipe.

Brandied Cheese Mix

1 pound Cheddar cheese, room temperature
¼ cup brandy
¼ cup butter, room temperature
¼ cup heavy cream
¼ teaspoon nutmeg
¼ teaspoon dry mustard
½ cup pitted black olives

In a food processor or blender combine all the ingredients, except the olives, and blend until smooth. Add the olives and pulse a few times to blend. Serve with slices of hot French bread, melba toast or an assortment of crisp crackers. Makes 10 to 12 servings.

Alii Caviar Cream

1 lemon
½ cup sour cream, room temperature
12 ounces cream cheese, room temperature
¼ cup chopped green onion
½ teaspoon salt
Curly lettuce leaves
1 jar (2 oz.) caviar, well chilled

Remove the zest from the lemon and finely chop the zest. Squeeze the juice from the lemon. In a food processor or blender combine the sour cream, cream cheese, green onions, lemon zest, lemon juice and salt; process until well blended. Line a pretty mold with plastic wrap. Pour the cheese mixture into the mold, cover and refrigerate until very firm, overnight is best. When ready to serve, line a plate with the curly lettuce leaves and place the mold top side down on the plate. Unmold the cream and remove the plastic wrap very carefully. Spoon caviar on the top of the cream mold. Serve with freshly made melba toast. Makes 10 to 12 servings.

Gingery Pickled Vegetables

2 cans large whole mushrooms
2 cans large pitted black olives
1 large head cauliflower
2 cucumbers
2 carrots
½ cup fresh grated ginger
1 Hawaiian red chili pepper, seeded and finely chopped
½ cup sugar
¼ cup vinegar
¼ cup water
1 teaspoon salt

Drain the canned mushrooms and olives. Cut cauliflower into florets and blanch for 2 to 3 minutes. Peel cucumbers and cut into ½-inch thick slices. Peel carrots and cut into 1-inch lengths and round off corners. Blanch for 3 minutes. Combine mushrooms, olives, cauliflower, cucumbers, carrots, ginger and chili pepper. In a small saucepan combine sugar, vinegar, water and salt and bring to a boil. Reduce heat and simmer until sugar dissolves. Pour vinegar mixture over the vegetables and chill for several hours or overnight to two days, stirring the mixture several times. Makes 12 to 16 servings.

Spiced Macadamia Nut Sauce
with Vegetables

½ cup minced onion
2 tablespoons oil
1 can (3½ oz.) macadamia nuts
1 can (12 oz.) coconut milk
¼ teaspoon crushed red chili peppers
2 teaspoons sugar
½ teaspoon salt
2½ tablespoons lemon juice
   Selection of vegetables:
      Bean sprouts, blanched and chilled
      Carrot sticks or curls
      Chinese peas, blanched and chilled
      Cauliflower florets
      Broccoli florets
   Lettuce leaves

In a skillet saute onion in oil until soft. In a food processor or blender grind macadamia nuts into a smooth paste. Add macadamia nut butter, coconut milk, red chili peppers, sugar, salt and lemon juice to the skillet. Cook until hot and well blended, about 15 minutes. Cool. When ready to serve arrange vegetables on lettuce leaves and place a bowl of the Spiced Macadamia Nut Sauce in the center. Makes about 8 servings.

Eggplant Dip (Vegetarian Caviar)

2 large eggplants
1 large Maui onion, chopped
½ cup olive oil
¼ cup fresh lemon juice
½ cup chopped parsley
¼ cup chopped fresh mint
3 cloves garlic, chopped
1 tablespoon dried oregano or 2 tablespoons fresh oregano, chopped
Salt and pepper to taste
Curly lettuce
Tomato wedges
Lemon wedges
Greek olives or black olives
Toasted Pita Points

Preheat overn to 350F. Cut eggplants in half lengthwise. Score the skin of the eggplants and bake for 30 to 50 minutes or until soft. Check after 30 minutes on the texture. If it seems soft remove from the oven at that time. Remove the skin from the eggplant and discard. Combine eggplant, onion, olive oil, lemon juice, parsley, mint, garlic, oregano, salt and pepper; stir until well blended. Chill. When ready to serve line the serving dish with curly lettuce. Place the eggplant dip in the center and surround with tomato wedges, lemon wedges and olives. Accompany with Toasted Pita Points. Makes 12 to 16 servings.

Toasted Pita Points

Cut pita bread into eight pieces and separate. Place on a baking sheet and bake at 325F. for 5 minutes. Place the hot pita points in a basket and serve with Eggplant Dip.

Humus (Chick Pea Spread)

  3 cups chick peas, freshly cooked or canned
  2 teaspoons salt
  4 cloves garlic, minced
  ½ cup olive oil
  ⅓ cup fresh lemon juice
  ¼ cup Italian parsley or Chinese parsley
  3 tablespoons chopped mint leaves

In a food processor combine all the ingredients; blend well. Chill. Serve with toasted pita points and fresh vegetable slices. Makes 10 to 12 servings.

Pepperoni and Maui Onion Dip

  4 ounces pepperoni, cut into 1-inch cubes
  1 Hawaiian red chili pepper, seeded and coarsely
     chopped
  2 tablespoons fresh basil
  ¼ cup chopped Maui onion
  2 cloves garlic
  2 tablespoons sun dried tomatoes
  1 package (8 oz.) cream cheese, room temperature

In a food processor combine pepperoni, Hawaiian red chili pepper and basil and chop coarsely. Add onion, garlic and sun dried tomatoes; process until well blended. Add cream cheese and process until blended. Serve at room temperature with vegetables, chips or an assortment of crisp crackers. This may be made several days ahead and chilled. Makes 8 to 10 servings.

Blue Hawaii Cheese Dip

½ pound Danish blue cheese
1 package (8 oz.) cream cheese, softened
½ cup mayonnaise
1 teaspoon horseradish
1 tablespoon Worcestershire sauce
2 tablespoons brandy (optional)

Combine all the ingredients in a food processor; blend well. Chill. Serve with crisp crackers. Makes 8 to 10 servings.

Aloha Spinach Dip

1 pound fresh spinach or 1 package (10 oz.) frozen spinach
2 cups sour cream
1 cup mayonnaise
1 package (.9 oz.) vegetable soup mix
1 cup chopped watercress
½ cup chopped Maui onion
1 teaspoon dill
2 cloves garlic, minced
1 teaspoon oregano
1 tablespoon finely chopped fresh basil
   Salt to taste

Blanch spinach and coarsely chop; drain well. Combine all ingredients; blend well. Chill. Serve with assorted fresh vegetables. Makes 10 to 12 servings.

Tropical Fruit Medley

½ cup curacao (orange liqueur)
4 cups cubed fresh pineapple
2 cups seedless green grapes, halved
2 cups fresh strawberries or 1 package (12 oz.)
  frozen whole strawberries, partially thawed
  Sprigs of mint

Pour curacao on pineapple and green grapes; toss. Chill.
Slice strawberries. Just before serving stir strawberries into
pineapple mixture. Garnish with mint. Makes 8 to 10
servings.

Ginger Stuffed Lychees

1 can (1 lb., 4 oz.) lychees
1 pkg. (3 oz.) cream cheese
1½ teaspoons fresh lemon juice
½ teaspoon sugar
2 tablespoons finely chopped crystallized ginger
6 maraschino cherries, thinly sliced

Drain lychees. Beat together cream cheese, lemon juice and
sugar until fluffy. Stir in crystallized ginger. Stuff lychees
with cream cheese mixture. An easy way to do this is with
a piping bag. Top each lychee with a slice of cherry. Makes
20 to 24.

Carpaccio

1½ pounds fat free top round steak
¼ cup Balsamic vinegar
½ cup olive oil
4 cloves garlic, minced
1 Maui onion, finely chopped
1 cup finely chopped parsley
¼ cup capers, rinsed and dried
1 tablespoon Hawaiian salt
1 teaspoon freshly ground black pepper
1 loaf hot French bread, sliced

Slice steak paper thin and pound on a dampened surface with a meat pounder. Place pieces of beef on a large platter barely overlapping each slice. Combine vinegar, olive oil and garlic. When ready to serve sprinkle beef with onion, parsley, capers, salt and pepper. Shake the oil mixture and sprinkle over beef. Fold each piece of meat into fourths and place on the French bread. Serve at once. Makes 8 servings.

Seviche

1½ pounds sea scallops
1 pound firm white fish, cut into 1-inch squares
  Lemon, lime or a combination of lemon and lime juice, to cover the fish
1 bell pepper, coarsely chopped
1 Maui onion, cut into small wedges
2 tomatoes, peeled, seeded and cut into wedges
1 to 2 hot red chili peppers, seeded and finely chopped
1 tablespoon Worcestershire sauce
1 cup chopped parsley

Combine all ingredients, except the parsley, and marinate overnight. When ready to serve drain off the liquid and sprinkle chopped parsley over the top. Serve with fresh hot French bread. Makes 10 to 12 servings.

ALOHA PUPUS

Bird of Paradise

Crab Siu Mai

1 pound cooked crab, shredded
½ pound ground pork
¼ cup soy sauce
2 tablespoons dry sherry
1 tablespoon sesame oil
1 can (8 oz.) water chestnuts, chopped
8 dried Chinese mushrooms, soaked, squeezed dry and chopped
¼ cup chopped green onion
1 tablespoon grated fresh ginger
1 egg, beaten
1 teaspoon salt
¼ teaspoon white pepper
30 dim sum wrappers

In a medium bowl combine all the ingredients, except dim sum wrappers; mix well. Place a tablespoon of the mixture in the middle of the wrapper. Gather sides of the wrapper around the filling, letting the wrapper pleat naturally. The top surface of the filling stays exposed. Squeeze the middle gently to shape dumpling. Keep covered until all are shaped. Place on steamer rack and steam for 15 to 18 minutes. Serve siu mai with a variety of dipping sauces. Makes 30.

Wrapper Dough

1½ cups cake flour
¾ cup boiling water

Mix flour and boiling water in a bowl with a spoon or in
a food processor. Knead the dough, when cool enough to
handle, until dough is smooth. Cover with a bowl and allow dough to rest for 20 to 30 minutes before shaping the
dough into a log. Cut the log into 30 pieces and roll into
thin circles about 3-inches in diameter. A pasta machine
is an easy way to prepare thin sheets of dough. Cover the
dough as you are working with it so it does not get too
dry to handle. Makes 30 dim sum wrappers (3-inches in
diameter).

Idea: Long strips of thin dough can be rolled, then cut into
3-inch squares for wun tun wrappers or 4-inch squares for
egg roll wrappers.

Plum Dipping Sauce

¼ cup Chinese plum sauce
¼ cup soy sauce
¼ cup Chinese style mustard

Combine plum sauce, soy sauce and mustard; blend well.
Makes ¾ cup.

Apricot Dipping Sauce

1 cup apricot preserves
1 tablespoon Chinese style mustard

In a small saucepan combine apricot preserves and
mustard. Heat, stirring frequently, until well blended.
Makes 1 cup.

Crispy Egg Rolls

½ pound boneless chicken
2 tablespoons grated fresh ginger
4 green onions, shredded
2 tablespoons oyster sauce
¼ cup dry sherry
½ pound cooked ham, cut in thin strips
12 dried Chinese mushrooms, soaked, squeezed dry
   and shredded
1 cup fresh spinach, cut into fine shreds
¼ pound Chinese peas (snow peas), remove strings
   and cut in thin strips
1 cup finely shredded Chinese cabbage
¼ cup chopped Chinese parsley
2 cups bean sprouts, cleaned and dried
2 tablespoons soy sauce
1 teaspoon sesame oil
1 egg
1 tablespoon water
24 (4-inch square) egg roll wrappers
   Oil for deep frying

Poach chicken; shred. In a medium bowl combine chicken, ginger, green onions, oyster sauce and 2 tablespoons of the sherry; blend well and set aside for 10 minutes. Combine chicken mixture, ham, Chinese mushrooms, spinach, Chinese peas, Chinese cabbage, Chinese parsley, bean sprouts, soy sauce, the remaining 2 tablespoons sherry and sesame oil; blend well. Beat together egg and water. Place 2 tablespoons of the chicken mixture in the corner of an egg roll wrapper and wrap like a parcel. Seal the edges with the egg wash. Heat oil to 375F. Fry a few egg rolls at a time in the hot oil until golden brown. Drain well on absorbent paper and continue frying the remaining rolls. Serve egg rolls with a variety of dipping sauces. Makes 24.

Char Siu Bao

1 tablespoon peanut oil
½ pound char siu (Chinese roast pork), finely
   chopped
2 tablespoons chopped green onion
¼ cup chicken stock
1 tablespoon oyster sauce
1 tablespoon soy sauce
1 teaspoon sesame oil
1 teaspoon honey
1 teaspoon grated fresh ginger
⅛ teaspoon white pepper
1 tablespoon cornstarch
1 tablespoon water
   Steamed Bread

Heat oil in a wok or heavy skillet and stir fry char siu for
1 minute. Stir in green onion, chicken stock, oyster sauce,
soy sauce, sesame oil, honey, ginger and white pepper; cook
for a few seconds. Blend together cornstarch and water to
make a smooth paste; stir into char siu mixture. Cook until
thickened. Set mixture aside to cool. Prepare Steamed
Bread. Roll the dough into 3-inch circles and place char
siu filling in the center of each. Gather the dough around
making small pleats as you do. Place the dough, gathered
side down on squares of waxed paper. Place bamboo
steamers over boiling water and place the char siu bao into
the steamers in a single layer. Cover and steam for 10
minutes. Char siu bao can be baked at 350F. for 20 minutes
Brush with egg white before baking. Makes 12.

Steamed Bread

   1 **cup lukewarm water**
   1 **tablespoon yeast**
   1 **tablespoon sugar**
2½ **cups flour**

Combine water, yeast and sugar; let sit for 3 to 4 minutes. In a food processor or by hand combine flour and yeast mixture. Knead until smooth and elastic. Cover the dough and allow to double in volume. When the dough has risen punch down and divide into 12 pieces. Shape each into a ball and place each ball on a square of waxed paper. Let rise for 10 minues. Proceed as directed in Char Siu Bao recipe.

Chinese Chicken in Lettuce Leaves

1 pound boneless chicken breasts
¼ cup oil
3 eggs
½ pound cooked ham, finely chopped
¼ cup chopped green onion
½ cup chopped water chestnuts
3 tablespoons rice wine or dry sherry
¼ cup soy sauce
1 teaspoon sesame oil
1 teaspoon hot bean paste
1 tablespoon cornstarch
1 tablespoon cold water
2 heads bibb lettuce, washed and dried
¼ cup chopped Chinese parsley

Remove skin from chicken and cut into ¼-inch cubes. In a wok or skillet heat 1 tablespoon of the oil. Beat the eggs and pour into the wok to make a thin omelet. Remove omelet from the pan and cut into thin strips. Add the remaining 3 tablespoons of the oil to the wok and stir fry chicken until almost cooked. Add the ham, green onion and water chestnuts; stir fry for a few minutes. Add rice wine, soy sauce, sesame oil and hot bean paste. Blend together cornstarch and water; stir into the chicken mixture. Cook a few minutes or until thickened. Add egg strips and toss lightly. Spread lettuce leaves on a large platter and place part of the chicken mixture on each leaf. Sprinkle with Chinese parsley. Fold the lettuce around the chicken and eat with your fingers. Makes 8 servings.

Tempura Party

This is a great way to spend an evening of fun eating and good conversation. Prepare a bowl of Tempura Batter and have it sitting in ice. Crumple paper towels on a tray for draining the deep fried food. Prepare Tempura Dipping Sauce and hot steamed rice. Present platters of seafood, meat and an assortment of vegetables cut into bite size pieces. Some ideas:

Scallops
Shrimp, shelled and deveined, leaving tails intact
Oysters and clams, removed from the shells
Beef, pork or lamb, cut in thin strips
Sweet potato slices
Green beans
Chinese peas (snow peas)
Green bell pepper strips
Fresh mushrooms or enoki mushrooms
Dried Chinese mushrooms, soaked and squeezed dry
and thinly sliced
Japanese eggplant, cut into fans and spread apart
Carrot slices
Green onions

Heat oil for deep frying in an electric wok to 375F. Increase the temperature as more food is added so that the heat remains hot enough for ingredients to brown in only a few minutes. Dip your selection into the Tempura Batter and let the excess batter drip off. Pull the ingredient across the edge of the batter bowl to remove any extra batter before placing in the hot oil. Fry until golden brown and crisp. Drain on the paper towels and continue cooking your selections. Serve individual plates with a bowl of Tempura Dipping Sauce and hot steamed rice, if desired.

Tempura Batter

1 cup cornstarch
1½ cups flour
1 egg
2 cups ice water

Mix together all the ingredients in a food processor or blender, or with a wire whisk. Blend until smooth. Place the bowl of batter in ice to keep it well chilled.

Tempura Dipping Sauce

1 cup soy sauce
½ cup chicken broth
½ cup mirin (Japanese sweet rice cooking wine)
2 tablespoons rice vinegar

Combine all the ingredients; blend well. Serve in small bowls either hot or cold. Makes 2 cups.

Sweet & Sour Fish for Chafing Dish

> 4 pounds firm white fish fillets
> ½ cup oil
> 2 tablespoons grated fresh ginger
> 2 cloves garlic, minced
> 1 tablespoon salt
> Sweet & Sour Sauce

Cut fish into 1-inch cubes. In a large bowl combine oil, ginger, garlic and salt. Add fish and marinate for 30 minutes. Prepare Sweet & Sour Sauce. Place fish on a platter that fits in a steamer or stack a number of steamers over a wok with 1-inch of water. When the water has come to a boil, steam the fish for 10 minutes. Place the cooked fish in a chafing dish and pour the Sweet & Sour Sauce over the top. Serve with crisp fried wun tun wrappers, if desired. Makes 12 to 16 servings.

Sweet & Sour Sauce

> 1½ cups rich chicken or fish stock
> ½ cup soy sauce
> ¼ cup sherry
> 2 tablespoons vinegar
> 2 tablespoons sugar
> ¼ cup chopped green onion
> 2 tablespoons grated fresh ginger
> 2 tablespoons hot bean paste
> ¼ teaspoon white pepper
> 2 tablespoons cornstarch
> ¼ cup cold water
> ½ cup julienned carrots
> ½ cup julienned green onions
> ½ cup julienned celery

In a sauce pan combine chicken stock, soy sauce, sherry, vinegar, sugar, green onion, ginger, hot bean paste and white pepper. Bring to a boil. Blend together cornstarch and water; mix into the hot sauce and stir over low heat until thickened. Add the vegetables and keep warm while the fish is steaming.

Wiki Wiki Buffet Fondue

1 pound Swiss cheese, coarsely grated or
shredded
2 tablespoons flour
2 cloves garlic, minced
1 cup Chablis wine
Dash of white pepper
Dash of ground nutmeg

Place the cheese and flour in a plastic or paper bag and shake until cheese is well coated with flour. In a fondue dish combine garlic, wine, white pepper and nutmeg; heat until almost boiling, but do not boil. Gradually add the cheese to the wine over low heat, stirring constantly, until cheese is melted. If the mixture is too thick at any time add a small amount of heated wine. Serve with cubes of French bread, slices of cold rolled ham, salami, pepperoni and vegetables cut in bite-size pieces. Have fondue forks or bamboo skewers ready for spearing. Makes 12 to 16 servings.

Maikai Sandwiches in a Bread Basket

> 1 very large loaf whole grain bread
> 10 to 12 slices white bread
> 10 to 12 slices rye bread
> 10 to 12 slices whole wheat bread
> Butter, room temperature
> Mayonnaise
> Cucumber, thinly sliced
> Watercress, cut into 1-inch lengths
> Dijon style mustard
> Maui onion, thinly sliced
> 4 slices Swiss cheese
> Horseradish
> Radishes, thinly sliced
> Alfalfa sprouts

Cut off top third of the large loaf of bread; set top aside. Hollow out bread. Save center of the bread for making bread crumbs, if desired. Remove crusts from slices of bread. Lightly butter all the bread slices. Spread mayonnaise on the white bread; top with cucumbers, watercress and another slice of bread. Spread Dijon style mustard on rye bread; top with Maui onions, Swiss cheese and another slice of bread. On the whole wheat slices spread with a very light layer of horseradish; top with radishes, alfalfa sprouts and another slice of bread. Cut sandwiches into quarters and place in the bread basket. Place the top of the bread in place and chill until ready to use. Makes 25 to 30 servings.

Stuffed Tomatoes Kahala

8 ripe tomatoes
1 cup Pesto Sauce
2 cups orzo (rice shaped Greek pasta)
½ pound small shrimp, shelled and cleaned

Scoop out tomatoes; chill. Prepare the Pesto Sauce well ahead of time and refrigerate. In a large pot bring 4 quarts salted water to a boil. Add the orzo and cook until just tender, about 10 minutes. Combine orzo, shrimp and Pesto Sauce; mix well. Fill the tomato shells with orzo mixture. Refrigerate until ready to serve. Makes 8 servings.

Pesto Sauce

1 cup fresh basil leaves
1 cup fresh spinach leaves, washed and dried
¼ cup freshly grated Parmesan cheese
4 cloves garlic
2 tablespoons pine nuts
½ cup olive oil
1 teaspoon salt
1 teaspoon pepper

Combine all the ingredients in a food processor and process until well blended. Place in a jar, top with a little oil, and cover tightly. Refrigerate until ready to use.

SUNSET DESSERTS
AND DRINKS

Protea

Minted Chocolate Sunset

4 ounces unsweetened chocolate
1 cup butter, softened
2 cups sifted powdered sugar
4 eggs, beaten
2 teaspoons vanilla
½ teaspoon peppermint extract
¼ cup chopped macadamia nuts (optional)

In a small saucepan over low heat melt chocolate. In a food processor or blender combine melted chocolate, butter and powdered sugar; blend until smooth. Add eggs, vanilla and peppermint extract; blend well. Spoon mixture into paper baking cups placed in muffin tins. Sprinkle with macadamia nuts, if desired. Freeze until firm. Makes 12.

Kona Cafe Brulot

¼ cup sugar
1 vanilla bean or 1 tablespoon vanilla
  Zest of 1 orange
2 cups brandy
8 cups hot strong Kona coffee

Combine sugar and vanilla bean in a heat proof bowl; add orange zest. Heat the brandy very carefully over low heat, add to the sugar mixture and ignite, stirring constantly. Add the hot coffee. Serve at once. Makes 20 demitasse servings.

Grand Marnier Chocolate Mousse

 4 eggs, separated
¾ cup sugar
 6 ounces semi-sweet chocolate
¼ cup strong Kona coffee
¼ cup Grand Marnier
¾ cup unsalted butter
   Pinch of salt
   Orange Cream
   Thin strips orange zest

In a large bowl beat together egg yolks and sugar until light and fluffy. In a heavy pan combine chocolate, coffee, Grand Marnier and butter. Cook over low heat until chocolate melts. Add chocolate mixture to the egg yolks and beat lightly until well blended. Cool to room temperature. Beat the egg whites with the salt until they hold firm peaks. Fold the egg whites into the chocolate mixture. Place in individual serving dishes and chill. When ready to serve, top with a dollop of Orange Cream and a few strips of orange zest. Makes 4 to 6 servings.

Orange Cream

1 cup heavy cream
2 tablespoons sugar
2 teaspoons Grand Marnier

Whip the heavy cream until it holds firm peaks. Beat in sugar and Grand Marnier. Serve with Grand Marnier Chocolate Mousse.

Guava Chiffon Cake

    3 cups cake flour
    2 cups sugar
    1 teaspoon salt
    4 teaspoons baking powder
    ¾ cup oil
    7 eggs, separated
    ½ cup water
    ½ cup guava nectar concentrate
    ½ teaspoon cream of tartar
       Guava Icing

Preheat oven to 325F. Sift together flour, 1½ cups of the sugar, salt and baking powder. Make a well in the flour mixture and add oil, egg yolks, water and nectar; beat until smooth. Beat egg whites with cream of tartar until soft peaks form. Add the remaining ½ cup of the sugar gradually, beating until egg whites are stiff. Gently fold flour mixture into egg whites, until just blended. Pour into ungreased tube pan. Bake for 1 hour. Immediately turn pan upside down on a cake rack and let stand until cool. Remove from pan. Spread with Guava Icing. Makes 12 servings.

Guava Icing

    3 tablespoons butter
    2 cups powdered sugar
    ¼ cup guava nectar concentrate
    ⅓ cup chopped macadamia nuts (optional)

Cream butter; gradually add powdered sugar and beat until fluffy. Add nectar. Continue to beat until icing is smooth and stiff. Spread icing on Guava Chiffon Cake. Sprinkle with macadamia nuts, if desired.

Macadamia Apple Squares

½ cup butter, softened
1 cup sugar
3 eggs
2 cups graham cracker crumbs
½ cup flour
2 teaspoons baking powder
1½ teaspoons cinnamon
½ teaspoon ground allspice
½ teaspoon salt
1 cup milk
2 tart apples, grated
1 jar (3½ oz.) chopped macadamia nuts
1 teaspoon vanilla
Powdered sugar

Preheat oven to 350F. Grease and flour a 9-inch square baking pan. In a large bowl beat together butter and sugar until creamy. Add eggs, one at a time, beating well after each addition. Combine graham cracker crumbs, flour, baking powder, cinnamon, allspice and salt. Stir graham cracker mixture and milk into butter mixture; mix until well blended. Stir in apples, macadamia nuts and vanilla. Pour into prepared pan and bake for 40 to 45 minutes or until wooden pick inserted in center comes out clean. Dust with powdered sugar. Makes 12 servings.

Coconut Puffs

1   **can (12 oz.) coconut milk**
¼   **cup butter**
1   **cup flour**
4   **eggs**
½   **cup shredded coconut, lightly toasted·**
    Oil for deep frying

Heat coconut milk in a saucepan. Add butter and bring
to a boil. Add the flour all at once. Stir rapidly, until batter leaves the sides of the pan. Remove from heat and beat
in one egg at a time. Stir in the toasted coconut. Heat oil
to 375F. Drop batter by teaspoons into hot oil and cook
until golden brown. Drain on absorbent paper towels.
Sprinkle with powdered sugar, if desired. Serve warm.
Makes 8 to 10 servings.

Lemon Tarts

1½ cups sugar
½ cup unsalted butter
½ cup fresh lemon juice
2 tablespoons finely chopped lemon zest
6 eggs, well beaten
24 baked Tart Shells (recipe page 31)
Sprigs of mint
Lemon twists

In the top of a double boiler combine sugar, butter, lemon juice and lemon zest. Over simmering water cook and stir the mixture until the sugar melts. Beat the eggs and slowly strain into the hot lemon mixture, stirring constantly, until the mixture thickens, about 15 to 20 minutes. When thickened remove from the heat and chill in a covered dish. The lemon curd will thicken as it chills. This may be made several days before using. Fill the tart shells with the lemon mixture and garnish with a sprig of fresh mint and a small twist of lemon. Makes 24.

Kona Coffee Ice

2 cups very strong Kona coffee
1 cup Hawaiian Cane Syrup
½ cup Kahlua coffee liqueur
½ cup heavy cream

Combine Kona coffee, Hawaiian Cane Syrup and Kahlua; blend well. Pour into a plastic or metal ice tray. Freeze for several hours. Remove from the freezer, break up the coffee mixture and blend until very light and fluffy. Return to the freezer for another hour or two. Place 4 glasses in the freezer. When ready to serve whip the heavy cream until it holds firm peaks. Spoon the coffee ice into the frosted glasses and top each serving with a dollop of whipped cream. Sprinkle a small amount of ground coffee over the top, if desired. Makes 4 servings.

Malasadas

2 medium potatoes
½ cup water
1 teaspoon sugar
2 pkg. (¼ oz. each) yeast
4 teaspoons salt
1 cup sugar
3 tablespoons butter
8 eggs, beaten
4 cups flour
    Oil for deep frying
    Sugar

Cook potatoes until soft; mash. Cool to luke warm. Stir
in water, sugar, yeast and 1 teaspoon of the salt. Let rise
for 30 minutes. Combine sugar and butter; beat. Add eggs,
4 cups of the flour and potato mixture; mix well. Mix in
remaining flour and the remaining 3 teaspoons of the salt.
Knead for 15 to 20 minutes. Let rise in a warm place until
double in volume. Heat oil to 375F. Drop dough by
tablespoons into hot oil and fry until golden brown, turning once. Drain on absorbent paper. Place sugar in a paper
bag and add fried malasadas; shake well to coat. Serve
warm.

Mauna Kea Brandy Drink

4 cups milk
1 vanilla bean
1½ cup sugar
   Pinch of salt
6 ounces semi-sweet chocolate, chopped
½ cup heavy cream
2 cups strong hot coffee
1½ cups brandy
2 tablespoons finely chopped macadamia nuts (optional)

In a saucepan combine milk, vanilla bean, sugar and salt and bring to a simmer. Remove from heat and add the chocolate; let stand until the chocolate melts. Stir well and allow to cool. When ready to serve whip the heavy cream until it holds firm peaks. Add the coffee and the brandy to the chocolate mixture. Serve in glass mugs or glasses. Top each serving with a dollop of whipped cream. Sprinkle with macadamia nuts, if desired. Makes 8 to 10 servings.

Kahlua Stinger

1¾ ounces Kahlua coffee liqueur
¾ ounces white creme de menthe
½ cup crushed ice

Put all ingredients into a blender container, cover and blend well. Strain. Makes 1 drink.

INDEX

INDEX

INDEX